PR

DON'T BE A FUCKING DICK

"Can you imagine the nerve of a guy that steals my material for his book, then asks me to write a recommendation? While I admire Milstein's chutzpah, I like DBAFD even more—he's mastered some of the required reading syllabus and made it his own. His treatment of the Trust Equation is deft, and his flippant style belies a clear amount of solid, clear thinking. If I disagreed with anything, I can't remember it."

–CHARLIE GREEN, AUTHOR OF *THE TRUSTED ADVISOR* AND
CREATOR OF THE TRUST EQUATION

Madeline,
Thank you for your
contributions to my beliefs
on leadership. We've seen
a lot of stuff together, some
of it making its way into
this book.
I love our friendship!
Howie

ABOUT THE ANNOYING AUTHOR

HOWIE MILSTEIN decided early in his career to question conventional thinking and seek the truth that is rooted in unbiased observation. As the world of medicine tries to evolve toward a system of evidence-based care, so Howie believes that it's more meaningful to live an evidence-based life and lead evidence-based communities.

As the Twin Cities' first personal trainer in the 1980's, Howie found that available resources that promoted certain ways of motivating his clients did not resonate with his observations. Spawned from this curiosity to learn the bases of the human condition was a passion that guided his studies and leadership principles. These principles have been implemented in many roles since his personal training days, including over 25 years managing teams in the medical device industry, with titles including Distributor, National Sales Manager, Sr. Vice President of Sales, Chief Operating Officer, President, and The Gangster of Love (his favorite). Now reinvented as a leadership consultant, author, and career coach, his titles are Vocational Irritant and Provocateur. Proudly annoying, Howie has many victims including his clients, audiences, community stakeholders, and nonprofit agencies and board members.

A strong adherent to the ideas of Self Determination Theory—including the principles of autonomy, mastery, and purpose—Howie learned that acquiring an understanding of motivation was only half the battle. In order to optimize culture, employee engagement, and predictable outcomes, he had to become deeply introspective and choose the best leadership style to nurture innovation, passion, and growth. When he stopped taking himself so seriously, things got better. Much better.

As the CEO/Provocateur with the Institute to Stop Taking Yourself So Seriously!, Howie's message is that, while there are myriad options to attempt cultural change in organizations, perhaps the only necessary thing is for individuals to seriously manage their egos. Jobs and careers aren't just for economic sustenance, rather they are a means to access and contribute to healthy communities where individuals are emotionally bolstered, challenged, and valued.

Howie takes a lighthearted approach to life and brings that to his writing and speaking style. He encourages questions and spirited discussions in order to challenge dysfunctional paradigms, to which he has developed a serious allergy. Believing that change is not possible without discomfort, Howie ensures that those in his sphere will never have so much fun while being encouraged to step outside their comfort zones.

Howie holds degrees in biochemistry and exercise physiology, as well as certifications in Intrinsic Coaching (Totally Coached/Intrinsic Solutions International) and as a Job and Career Transition Coach. He has a wife and three adult children with minds of their own. Residing in Plymouth, Minnesota, Howie likes to golf, garden, ride motorcycles, and keep himself in reasonable physical (and mental) condition. He is a strong advocate for community and has held many nonprofit volunteer leadership positions. He is addicted to entrepreneurism and new ideas, which drives his wife and friends crazy.

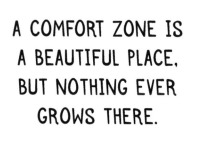

A COMFORT ZONE IS
A BEAUTIFUL PLACE,
BUT NOTHING EVER
GROWS THERE.

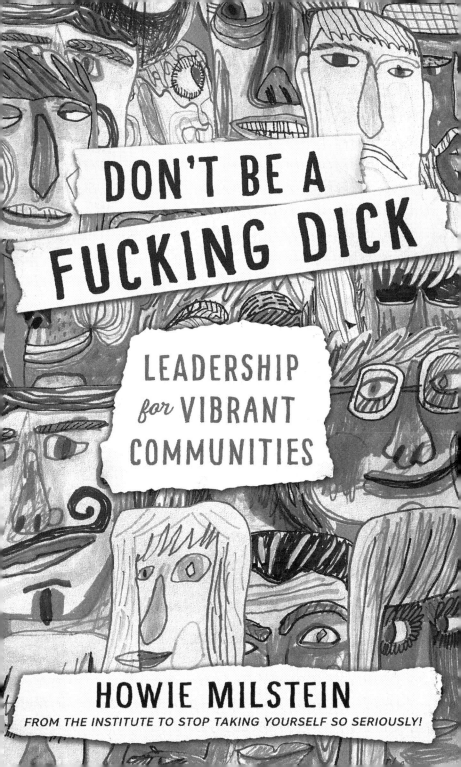

DON'T BE A FUCKING DICK

LEADERSHIP *for* VIBRANT COMMUNITIES

HOWIE MILSTEIN

FROM THE INSTITUTE TO STOP TAKING YOURSELF SO SERIOUSLY!

DON'T BE A FUCKING DICK

Leadership for Vibrant Communities

By Howie Milstein, Provocateur

From The Institute to Stop Taking Yourself So Seriously!

CONTENTS

PIQUING YOUR CURIOSITY 9

ONE: Just This Side of the Monkey Cage 13

TWO: Gotta Have It! 21

THREE: Community Vibrancy 31

FOUR: If I Say I'm the Most Trustworthy, I'm Likely Not 39

FIVE: The New Power Skills 45

SIX: Sorry, Some Math Is Required 57

SEVEN: Who's the Fairest? 69

EIGHT: The 'Ol One-Two 85

NINE: Am I, or Am I Not? 95

TEN: Stop Me Before I Write Again 99

ACKNOWLEDGMENTS: It Takes a Village, er, Community! 103

INVITATION:
Piquing Your Curiosity

If you are a consultant in the area of employee engagement, leadership development, or organizational culture, STOP READING RIGHT NOW! In an act of utter benevolence, I'm giving you advance warning that the guidance in this book, if heeded, could put you out of business. Bummer for you, because my publisher has dissuaded me from offering a money-back guarantee on book purchases. Hopefully you'll agree that it either looks great on your bookshelf or in your garbage can, in which case your trash collector might find it and re-gift it to their boss. If your waste hauler is back in a couple weeks with a beaming smile on their face, consider your tossing the book a great success.

Look, consultants have created myriad assessments, schemes, workshops, and programs designed to placate organizations into believing they're doing great work to create great leaders and great cultures. Maybe because they are afraid to address the elephant in the room, or there weren't enough billable hours, they've simply skirted the one strategy necessary to bring joy, gratification, and engagement to our teams, offices, congregations, warehouses, manufacturing facilities, and all other gatherings of people collectively known as COM-MUNITIES. And that is the aim of this book—to create more functional communities where members are thriving, contributing, and happy.

Empirical evidence over decades has shown that we haven't moved the engagement (a.k.a. happiness) bar at all, even with the billions of dollars we've spent trying. I'm not going to do much, if any, review of data here—if you're interested, just go to gallup.com or Google "why the workplace sucks." I've spent so much time watching the data mount up and working fruitlessly to influence change, that I've become baffled about our collective inability to simply try better tactics. Must all our strategies include drawn-out consulting arrangements with handsome fees? No.

At this point, I invite those of you who have ventured this far into the book to exercise your privilege to stop reading. In fact, if you take to heart the advice found on the cover, you've pretty much gotten the message. However, knowing what to do, why you want to do it, and actually doing it takes a bit of heightened consciousness. So if you're feeling game, persevere.

As evolved as we think we are, none of us change easily or quickly. We typically spend the majority of our lives acquiring credentials like education and skills, but don't often intentionally focus on building emotional intelligence. I know it's not easy, but if I didn't know that we have the capacity to change, I wouldn't have wasted my time writing this. Trust me, it's not a get-rich-quick scheme.

Lest you believe that, owing to the title of this book, it is directed specifically to males, I proclaim that the term "dick" is gender neutral, applicable to anyone regardless of their gender identification. In fact, I have personally encountered many dicks endowed with female DNA, and I imagine that you, reader, could name one woman or a dozen who you've thought about in these—and more colorful—terms.

This book takes a shot at provoking readers into choosing to act with more emotional intelligence. It will work well for people who have the courage to seek, and internalize, honest feedback and acquire more self-awareness. It's also a great gift for the person, boss, or politician in your life who's a charter member of the dickhood and doesn't either realize it or bother to care. Either way, I'm hopeful that it will sell somewhere between 12 and a million copies.

Read on...

CHOOSE YOUR OWN CAPTION

a After failing to receive an explanation of the word "address," the artist ran with his own interpretation.

b The artist's attempt to set a world record for first class postage.

c Finally, the elephant in the room gets addressed. Annoying to all, including the elephant.

d This time, the mail carrier justifiably deserves a big tip.

ONE:
Just This Side of the Monkey Cage

We humans (already with the complicated syntax, as I guess "us humans" ain't correct) are delightfully complex yet surprisingly simple. Nobody thinks more highly of our presently evolved state than ourselves, but I suspect that if you asked dogs, apes, or other denizens of the rainforest, they might think a bit less of us. Other creatures are all too aware of our imperfections, idiosyncrasies, and capacity to believe just about anything.

On the side of believing we have a modicum of control, there's a school of thought that says we are free to choose our behavior. Otherwise known as free will, it might make us feel good about giving ourselves credit for the good things we do. It also could serve as the basis for blaming and judging others for the bonehead things they do. Heaven forbid, though, that we hold ourselves accountable for our own misdeeds.

Then there is a belief that we're a product of our environment and upbringing. We learn things, consciously and subconsciously, about what to think and how to behave from friends, neighbors, parents, classmates, teachers, the media, and Little Johnny, the self-purported expert from second grade who taught us how to propagate the species. This way of thinking absolves us of guilt for doing bad things, ascribing blame to outside circumstances beyond our control and relieving us of the annoying accountability for being less than amazing. If we're not aware that we are profoundly influenced by our environment, we are left to take credit for an uncanny ability to make some pretty rotten choices.

It's ridiculous to think that there are only two ways to look at the influences underlying human behavior. We're way too complicated for that. I spent almost three decades in the world of healthcare—marketing, selling, and servicing surgical devices. On the clinical side of that industry, it was important to make decisions based on the evidence at hand, observing the outcomes achieved through the various treatments administered. The fact that choices are increasingly made based predominantly (solely?) on economic outcomes is beside the point (and probably a commentary on our shameless healthcare system, but that is for another book) as the vast majority of clinicians try to employ evidence-based medicine as their modus operandi.

I like to think I'm striving to lead an evidence-based life and tried valiantly to lead evidence-based businesses, but I don't see this methodology commonly employed in society. Rather, we default to conventional thinking, making choices based on historical standards or the wisdom of experts and consultants. The further an expert travels to deliver a message, the more credible they are, as it surely isn't possible to have enough experts close to home. Tales of people cutting the ends off hams prior to baking because that's how their grandmothers did it, only to find out their elders did this because archaic ovens weren't large enough to accommodate a full-sized ham, are illustrative. Likewise, when one of my predecessors in the leadership ranks suggested I avoid getting "too close to my people" when assuming a supervisory role, this proved to be likewise grounded in what I came to understand as lacking enlightenment.

WE DEFAULT TO CONVENTIONAL THINKING, MAKING CHOICES BASED ON HISTORICAL STANDARDS OR THE WISDOM OF EXPERTS AND CONSULTANTS.

History teaches us the value, and potential pitfalls, of challenging conventional thinking. When Galileo supported Copernicus's theory that the sun was the center of our universe with the planets revolving around it, opposition to his work was intense, including an Inquisition by the Roman Catholic Church. Of course, we all know how that turned out, with the Vatican finally admitting Galileo's theory was correct—350 years later. Thankfully we can now make mathematical sense of the calendar and accurately manage our seasonal intake of Vitamin D.

MOST OFTEN OUR BEHAVIOR IS HABITUAL, DICTATED BY PATTERNS WE'VE LEARNED OR OBSERVED IN THE PAST RATHER THAN BY CONSCIOUS CHOICES ABOUT HOW TO RESPOND IN THE PRESENT.

Since we are enamored of our conventional thinking, we're lucky when paradigm-busting is taught and encouraged. As a junior in college, I had the fortune to have a biochemistry professor who, in our very first class, introduced the concept of paradigm jumping. Referencing a pioneering book by Thomas Kuhn, *The Structure of Scientific Revolutions*, Professor Kirkwood essentially gave us permission to consider that everything he was about to teach us might be patently incorrect.

With all this talk about how we think, one could be led to believe we're fully aware of what's going on in our minds. As it turns out, we're wrong. Instead, we are creatures who often fly on autopilot, driven by subconscious and unconscious processes playing fast and loose with our heads. Most often our behavior is habitual, dictated by patterns we've learned or observed in the past rather than by conscious choices about how to respond in the present. The emotional center of the brain—known as the limbic system and comprised largely of the mass of gray matter known as the amygdala—processes everything we see, hear, and read, steering much of our behavior before rational analysis even gets a chance.

So much of our conduct is based on unrecognized perceptions of fear—fears our unconscious brains recognize as mortal that are, in fact, only uncomfortable. Our reactions to these deep fears are what matter as they often fail to lead to the best outcomes. Human actions are ingrained and habitual, meaning that we act without really thinking. Many habits serve us well such as those that inspire us to grab the bar of soap while showering, remember to turn the car off after parking it, and use a reasonably long stick when roasting marshmallows. Deep thinking isn't always necessary, but it sure comes in handy when you want to keep your dearly held relationships intact.

When left to their own devices, our brains don't always make the best decisions for us or others. How many times have we popped a handful of M&Ms in our mouths, having succumbed to the irresistible urge to eat something so sweet and colorful? The fact that we're trying to maintain a healthy weight, even lose a few pounds, is literally lost on us and before we know it, the family-size (which I submit should be rebranded as the fun-size) bag is history. Or how about when we yell at an employee, when a more measured response might have prevented that employee from shutting down for the next two weeks while using company time to write their resume? The literal costs of poor emotional control to commercial enterprise and the global economy are staggering.

We are also gaining more clarity on the cognitive biases we wake up with every day. Sometimes referred to as unconscious, implicit, cognitive, and confirmation biases, they cause us to default to the categorization of people and information in ways that are aligned with fears, such as fear of the other, fear of being wrong, or fear of paying too much for a new Volkswagen. These biases, which arise from our own social evolution, are adaptations etched into our automatic brain processes and help to explain tribalism and other -isms around culture, religion, and politics.

So when left unchecked by conscious thinking, our brain doesn't always operate so usefully. We are driven by perceptions of fear often based not in reality, but in evolutionary constructs that are no longer relevant, especially since the extinction of the Saber-Toothed Tiger, the T-Rex, and the Corvair. We default to tribalism, separating ourselves from others who don't look or sound like we do. If you're going to be a leader of humans, in addition to knowing how the brain is wired, it's helpful to know what inspires people and what turns them off. In other words, it's nice to understand how people are motivated and, consequently, de-motivated.

This book, essentially, is about thinking better as a path to becoming and behaving better. It's about seizing conscious control of the dysfunctional places our brains go and acting in ways that are more aligned with empirical evidence and our modern understanding of what people need and how they're motivated. And it's about giving us what we really want by giving others what they really need, and not pretending that our old conventions still hold true when we have solid evidence to the contrary. In sum, it's about emotional intelligence.

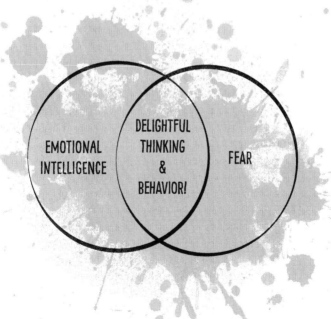

TWO:
Gotta Have It!

You're probably thinking to yourself, "Who does Howie think he is, telling me what I want?" Like it's not obvious to me and every other reader? Well, if we were so dang self-aware, we'd know everything about ourselves but, as I just suggested, we have a lot going on behind the curtain of awareness.

So what about letting Abraham Maslow tell us what we need? The vaunted American psychologist published his theory, known as the hierarchy of needs, in 1943 (which begs the question of whether he was aware of the impending invention of the smartphone because there isn't one to be found on his list).

In Maslow's framework, there are obvious physiological needs like air, water, sleep, shelter, pizza, and ice cream (okay, "food" but the rest pales in MY book, which this is). Seriously, many people on the planet do not have most of their basic physiological needs met and the bane of their existence is spent meeting them. Once we do have those needs met, we move into physical and emotional safety. Then we are free to pursue social needs like friendships, family, and intimacy. After social needs are met, we have needs of the ego like status, respect, and recognition. Ultimately, we seek self-actualization or the realization of our full potential as human beings. Sex is a need that could be explained by many levels within Abe's hierarchy, as we use it to meet physiological, intimacy, and self-esteem needs. It's a key part of our drive that, thankfully, helps propagate our species (some of whom are nice to have around).

Within Maslow's third level of social belonging are the friendships and other relationships that enrich us. To this level I would ascribe the term "community" as defined by any gathering of people, in the same time and at the same place, for any reason whatsoever. Included are households, places of worship, community centers, movie theaters, restaurants, Independence Day displays, football stadiums, and the workplace. Had Maslow known about current neuroscientific findings about the value of community, he might have put the importance of community right up there with pizza and ice cream. And I almost forgot—chocolate.

Social scientists and psychologists have been on board with the value of community for quite some time. Google "value of community quotes" and you'll see an endless number of people have weighed in. However, neuroscience is teaching us more about the value of community. In his book,

Social: Why Our Brains Are Wired to Connect, neuroscientist Matthew Lieberman suggests (according to my interpretation) that Maslow got his hierarchy wrong. Social needs belong at the very bottom of the pyramid, even more basic than food, water, and shelter because without social support, for instance, infants won't survive into adulthood and be able to provide for themselves. Says Lieberman, "Love and belonging might seem like a convenience we can live without, but our biology is built to thirst for connection because it is linked to our most basic survival needs."

One of my good friends has every right to be a social misfit as he grew up not having a very apparent social need at his disposal. His mother skedaddled from his father, himself, and three of his young brothers, excising a nurturing force from the household. Yet my friend is emotionally centered, a great father, a cherished friend to many, and a stalwart in our midst. When I asked him why he wasn't screwed up, he asserted that the community, such as friends' parents and inhabitants of the hockey rink, raised him and his siblings. They took over where his mother left off and, for the most part, none are worse for wear. The community provided many of his developmental needs.

...THE WORKPLACE IS GENERALLY BROKEN.

HOWIE'S HIERARCHY OF NEEDS
(In no particular rank):

- Pizza
- Wide Fairways
- Good Bicycle Shorts
- Color
- People Around Me

- Dental Floss
- Coffee
- Cinnamon Buns
- Costco
- Led Zeppelin
- Creatures With Wagging Tails

So if we're indeed hardwired to NEED social belonging, what does this say about the community that is the workplace? It says that we need workplaces that are conducive to the development of meaningful, authentic relationships where the most basic human needs are met. The workplace is noteworthy as the principle access point for communal interaction for many of us, especially given the amount of time we spend working or goofing off these days.

Chances are, by this point, you're thinking about a bad workplace culture (or ten) that you've experienced, and remembering how bad, de-energized, and emotionally deflated you felt at the end of the workday. It might have had something to do with bad exchanges you had with coworkers, bosses, vendors, or customers. Maybe there was some bullying or injustice that left you with the short end of the stick (like blame for something outside your control). Or maybe somebody took the credit for the awesome work you did, leaving you feeling unrecognized and unappreciated.

> *WE NEED WORKPLACES THAT ARE CONDUCIVE TO THE DEVELOPMENT OF MEANINGFUL, AUTHENTIC RELATIONSHIPS WHERE THE MOST BASIC HUMAN NEEDS ARE MET.*

Let me tell you a little secret: normal humans with normally developed brains CANNOT exist healthily in bad work cultures. Your brain simply won't allow it, no matter how much you try to talk yourself out of it or justify it because of a handsome paycheck. You feel bad, like you've been punched in the gut. By the way, neuroscientists say that this type of social pain is felt in the same part of the brain as physical pain. Ouch!

Despite decades-long efforts to improve business culture with virtually no change in employee engagement scores and a 70-plus percent disengagement in the workforce, it's fair to assert that the workplace is generally broken. Workers are either biding their time to collect paychecks or actively looking for better gigs. Great for the recruiters and career coaches out there, but a bummer for sustainable operations, customer satisfaction, and optimal profits. Turnover is high, with organizations such as Gallup reporting that bad bosses are a key driver of the impulse to seek better bosses.

WE MUST KNOW HOW TO TREAT PEOPLE AND MOTIVATE THEM IN WAYS THAT MEET THEIR INTRINSIC NEEDS.

Indeed, it's the busted relationships that are the root cause of most employee unease, as we are simply not equipped to deftly manage the social hurts that come with them. And my peers in the world of organizational consultancy are not meeting this issue head on. Though we are, occasionally, meeting for beer on Thursdays. Clearly, we know the state of the workplace, but knowing doesn't translate into making it the healthy community that we desperately need. To do this, we must know how to treat people and motivate them in ways that meet their intrinsic needs.

One way of understanding the principles of motivation is through the study of self-determination theory. This theory, essentially favoring the intrinsic versus extrinsic motives behind behavior, was most clearly derived by psychologists Edward Deci and Richard Ryan in the 1980s. The key elements of this theory include autonomy, mastery, and relatedness. If you thought it was money, you'd be wrong. For a fun lesson on motivation and self-determination theory, read the book *Drive*, a book I find so accurate I wish I'd written it myself, but Daniel Pink beat me to it.

Briefly, autonomy is the need to feel like you have some decision-making authority, the ability to be in control and responsible for your life, and able to thrive in the world. Mastery is the feeling that you can become really good, even expert, at things. This speaks to the need to continually face challenges, while meeting them provides a sense of personal growth. Relatedness is most simply defined as the psychological need to have relationships and a social outlet. Way more on the social thing is addressed later in this book.

Pink adds purpose to these motivators, which is about understanding why you were bred to be on this planet in the first place. You manifest your purpose by being able to make a difference and have a positive impact on others. Collectively, self-determinant needs and purpose are all intrinsic motives, rewards to our inner selves that are not material. Money, a readily understood extrinsic motivator and the answer that all sales reps believe they should give in job interviews, is not sustainably motivational and can, in fact, be demotivational.

> MONEY, A READILY UNDERSTOOD EXTRINSIC MOTIVATOR AND THE ANSWER THAT ALL SALES REPS BELIEVE THEY SHOULD GIVE IN JOB INTERVIEWS, IS NOT SUSTAINABLY MOTIVATIONAL.

If it's autonomy we want, it's unsolicited advice we don't. One of my greatest pet peeves, and source of dissonance in my children owing to occasionally differing parental styles, unsolicited advice is mainly about the advice giver's need to have their own worldview validated. It's rarely well-received and tends to shut down the best thinking in others. What looks like oppositional behavior, in people of any age, is maybe just an honest manifestation of an antagonistic relationship with unsolicited advice.

As the human condition is far more complex than I've suggested, we have a long way to go to map the complexities of the brain, human behavior, and the formation and elimination of habits. However, we must work with what we have if we want to drive better health and well-being in communities. Operating from an awareness of the human condition provides a foundation from which we can make some valuable changes.

THREE:
Community Vibrancy

Unlike many business books that promise better profits if only you put their ideas into action, the deliverables from the practices espoused here are healthier communities with happier people, peacefully co-existing differing ideas, productive collaborative efforts, disagreements resolved through compromise, less loneliness and despair, and yes, better employee engagement leading to stronger business operations and results.

THERE ARE A LOT OF LONELY PEOPLE INTERFACING ON SOCIAL MEDIA, NO MATTER HOW VAST THEIR NETWORK OF CONTACTS MAY BE.

Communities are comprised of people sharing common characteristics or values, whether they be nationality, race, religion, or the desire to beat a league rival. Families, neighborhoods, cities, congregations, political bodies, classmates, bowling teams, and coworkers are examples of community constituents. Maybe there's a marginal case for including social media "friends," although I question whether technology actually satisfies the basic human need for social connection. There are a lot of lonely people interfacing on social media, no matter how vast their network of contacts may be.

Facebook CEO Mark Zuckerberg often uses the word "community" when describing his Internet platform. He has his detractors though. Sandy Parakilas, an advisor to the Center for Humane Technology and a former Facebook employee, suggests that the company has not always treated online users with the respect a community deserves. He cites the lack of transparency about Russian interference in the 2016 U.S. elections as an example. If Facebook were a true community builder, Parakilas believes, it would have to prioritize the interests of its users. Instead, its business model is based on making money through surveillance advertising, which can be used to divide and manipulate people. To build a true community, according to Parakilas, Facebook would need to make money from things that build connection.

Another commentary comes from Jose Marichal, professor of political science at California Lutheran University. Marichal believes that it is problematic and potentially dangerous to think that social media creates community. The Facebook community, by itself, is a "synthetic community," which is no substitute for the real thing. A Facebook community is stripped of the relational elements found in real communities, where physical encounters add elements of personal intimacy.

I am convinced that digital media doesn't satisfy the basic social requirements, as articulated in Maslow's hierarchy, that people REALLY need in their communities.

While sharing common core values among its members might be a component of a functional community, I submit that while there might be substantial overlap, values are highly personal, and differing ones need to coexist without causing violent chasms. Unhealthy manifestations of differences and disagreements,

A FACEBOOK COMMUNITY IS STRIPPED OF THE RELATIONAL ELEMENTS FOUND IN REAL COMMUNITIES, WHERE PHYSICAL ENCOUNTERS ADD ELEMENTS OF PERSONAL INTIMACY.

such as those existing in today's political climate, produce the underlying stress, anxiety, and anger that pit neighbor against neighbor. Even sibling against sibling.

We need leaders to model and influence the behaviors that support physically and emotionally nurturing environments. For leaders, it's not only WHAT they say or do that matters, it's also HOW they speak and act. Style matters, maybe more than content, as it triggers emotions that help interpret meaning and intent. Words, in and of themselves, matter but are always subject to interpretation. People are inherently aware of sincerity and subsequently, insincerity; we're endowed with a so-called bullshit meter, and we deeply know when inauthenticity (or self-interest) is in our midst.

It is incumbent upon leadership to create viable and intimate relationships and establish the inherent and perhaps unspoken rule that meaningful relationships matter. True leadership represents a collaborative between leaders and other stakeholders, and how well leaders act influences the outcomes of communal goals.

> IT IS INCUMBENT UPON LEADERSHIP TO CREATE VIABLE AND INTIMATE RELATIONSHIPS AND ESTABLISH THE INHERENT AND PERHAPS UNSPOKEN RULE THAT MEANINGFUL RELATIONSHIPS MATTER.

The effects of dysfunctional leadership are apparent. Negative gossip, leaking of confidential information, high personnel turnover, and mutinies are all indications that meaningful relationships aren't de rigueur. Being on the high seas with a bunch of dudes for weeks on end calls for the most effective leadership, lest the leader become shark bait. Ernest Shackelton serves as a prime example of the kind of leader to foster the most functional of relationships among his men, successfully heading Antarctic expeditions in the early 1900s that required enduring the harshest of conditions that weaker teams succumbed to, literally with their lives.

At the root of all relationships, both personal and professional, is trust. Without trust it is difficult, if not impossible, to enjoy the intimacy that people need through their social connections. HEALTHY relationships are based on trusting that you won't be disregarded, hurt (emotionally or physically), embarrassed, shamed, ripped off, diminished, or improperly exploited. Don't confuse this kind of trust with predictability, where we some-times say that we trust a person to act inappropriately, illegally, or down-right selfishly. That is not the kind of trust that engenders healthy relationships and communities.

AT THE ROOT OF ALL RELATIONSHIPS IS TRUST.

Sure, it can be productive to predict people's known weaknesses, such as "you can trust that if Jimmy gets ahold of the company checkbook, he'll find a way to quickly drain the coffers," because this precaution ulti-mately serves the organization well. While "trust" is generally used as a synonym for confidence, belief, expectation, etc., using it as a predictor of negative traits is an appropriate use of the word in the English language. Just know that trust, in the context of relationships and this book, refers to the assurance of things like respect, integrity, strength, consideration, and loyalty.

Should we belabor the question of whether trust is a given or something that is earned? Some people will claim they start off trusting others and only

IN MY WORLD, TRUST IS EARNED, AND CONTINUALLY STRENGTHENED THROUGH ONGOING EVIDENCE THAT SOMEONE REMAINS WORTHY OF THAT TRUST.

lose trust through compelling evidence of misdeeds. I suggest this isn't really trust but blind optimism. I don't doubt that wishful, even magical, thinking can delude us into having a nice day. However, you're possibly setting yourself up for giving a lot of credit where it may not be due.

In my world, trust is EARNED, and continually strengthened through ongoing evidence that someone remains worthy of that trust. Subsequently, trust is lost through direct and empirical evidence. How is trust—the foundation upon which healthy relationships and communities are created—built and lost?

Keep reading...

Expansion through Sharing

Why reinvent the dang wheel? Learn from others' mistakes, perhaps the finest educational tools ever invented, and find yourself on a shortcut to success.

Inspiration and Motivation

In a community, someone—not always the same person and even occasionally you—is doing something amazing. This can inspire others to emulate this coolness and do things that contribute to the greater good.

HEALTHY COMMUNITY EXPERIENCE OFFERS MANY BENEFITS

Opportunity

Learn from others' successes, our second greatest educational tool, and use that knowledge for personal and communal growth.

Network of Support

Someone in the community is bound to meet a particular need you might have for service, advice, support, understanding, and ice cream.

Fun

All work and no play make for people with the personalities of toasters. Social activities are great for keeping spirits high. Research demonstrates that people who feel connected to others have fewer negative behavioral and emotional issues, including anxiety and depression. Loneliness actually has an adverse influence on physical health. Lonely people often live shorter lives, and hence eat less pizza.

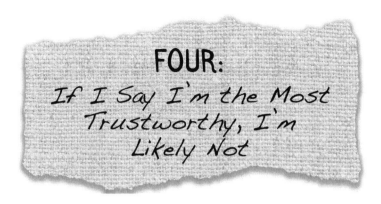

FOUR:
If I Say I'm the Most Trustworthy, I'm Likely Not

Having earned a degree in biochemistry—which by the way confers no credibility whatsoever in the world of organizational development, leadership training, or employee engagement—I have some awareness of the basic laws of thermodynamics. Even without this particularly useless credential, many people know that the First Law of Thermodynamics is that energy is neither created nor destroyed—it just kind of moves around.

Much to my chagrin, I cannot draw any thermodynamic parallels to the laws of trust. In fact, as stated by my own, henceforth-to-be-famous Howie's Law of Trust Dynamics, trust CAN be created and destroyed. And if you've been at all awake up to this point in your life, you've seen and felt the development and collapse of trust. No need for exhaustive, peer-reviewed studies with empirical evidence and front-page worthy conclusions here! The research lives in everyone's minds and hearts.

All leaders, whether those with fancy titles or those directing from the cheap seats, must understand the bases of trust. Years ago, I discovered a trust model, actually an equation that, upon scrutiny and interpretation, deeply resonated with my views. At the time, I didn't uncover the source of the equation, or delve into the creator's own perspectives. Rather, I stole it for my own speaking and presentation purposes. Feeling just a bit guilty and knowing that it belongs in these pages, I discovered the origins of the equation, reached out to Charles Green, one of the authors of the book, *The Trusted Advisor* (published by Free Press and, of course, available on Amazon), and received his gracious permission to exploit it for my own needs. And, mostly out of gratitude, I purchased the book to add to my own, impressive-looking shelves.

Still, I call on my own, independent interpretation of Charlie's Trust Model, which is:

$$T\,(TRUST) = \frac{C\,(CREDIBILITY) + R\,(RELIABILITY) + I\,(INTIMACY)}{S\,(SELF\text{-}INTEREST\;OR\;ORIENTATION)}$$

CREDIBILITY

According to my interpretation, credibility includes the expertise, experience, knowledge, skill, accomplishments, framed certificates, and other resume baloney someone brings to the party. They're the capabilities that people believe can help inform vision, strategy, and process that can yield a positive outcome. Credibility comes with age, education, a history of accomplishments, avoidance of bad press (or a good public relations agent), being lucky enough to have been recognized for past achievements, and even being authentically credible.

The credibility badge is kept by occasionally being right, admitting when you're wrong, and understanding your own strengths and weaknesses.

Credibility is compromised when it's obvious to others your claimed accomplishments were largely through the hard work and ideas of others. Taking credit, when credit is due, is best done quietly and with humility. Giving credit when it is due to others shows you recognize it takes a village to successfully manage the workplace, and while you genuinely take credit for your part in it, you're willing to share the glory. Thomas Edison didn't invent the light bulb alone, having surrounded himself with many capable contributors. He can duly take credit for vision and contributing to a fine result, but taking sole credit? Not legitimate.

The greatest destroyer of credibility? Lying. When facts aren't clearly verifiable, trust may be questioned but not radically compromised. However, when the facts are known, lying cannot only be disrespectful, it can irreversibly tarnish—or obliterate—trust.

RELIABILITY

Say what you'll do, then do what you said. One of the tenets of trust is simply being accountable for the stuff you're supposed to do, whether you've volunteered or it's part of a reasonable request and within the scope of your role in the community. Dropping the proverbial ball puts more work and responsibility on other community members, tarnishing their trust in you to carry your own weight.

Predictability is also a component of reliability. Thinking and behaving in ways that are consistent and in line with communal values and goals enables others to rely on you to be who you've demonstrated yourself to be in the past. Knowing how someone will take care of an issue, without being asked and without needing direction, enables the focus of energy to areas that do need attention, providing consistency and predictability in the function of a community.

Demonstrating strong work ethics are vital in sending the message that diligence is necessary throughout the organization; all people, even those with lofty titles, are required to make equivalent contributions. In a truly collaborative setting, everybody pulls their weight.

When leaders ask for data, ideas, reports, and other input to drive vision and strategy, and either don't acknowledge or act upon them, it is perceived as busy work or fake work, which inevitably contributes to distrust. People rely on their leaders to validate that their contributions are valuable and valued, and by extension, that they themselves are valuable and valued. There's nothing worse than spending two days on an elaborate analysis only to learn that it's been deemed irrelevant or unnecessary, let alone unread. We rely on our leaders to call on our strengths that contribute meaningfully to a common cause, and to challenge us to learn new skills that develop us into increasingly valuable contributors to the community.

INTIMACY

So far I've spared you, brave reader, long diatribes on the ideas I've presented. I'm not interested in building an exhaustive case, hitting you over the head with reams of data to convince you that we're going down the right path here. Instead, I'm asking you to have enough belief that there's validity in them thar' hills to inspire you to keep muscling through.

However, the next topic, the intimacy component of the Trust Model, is more complex and too challenging to conventional wisdom and common practice to gloss over. So, get yourself a fine glass of wine, enormous bowl of popcorn, gigantic stogie, or—if you reside in one of the growing number of areas where it's legal—a fat joint and immerse yourself in some ideas that only the courageous dare to consider. And if you're getting high where the authorities aren't entirely cool with it, it's none of my damn business.

MUCH TO TIFFANY'S DISMAY, HER BAD EXPERIENCE WITH THE EXPLOSIVE BOSS INCLUDED EXCESSIVE DRY CLEANING COSTS.

FIVE:
The New Power Skills

A couple years ago I was asked to speak to a group of women leaders in the municipal/public services sector. Because I am willing to put myself out there, subjecting people's sensibilities to any real or feigned credibility I show up with, I proposed the topic, "How to be more woman in your role as a female leader." Clearly, my direct experience in this topic was limited, but they nonetheless accepted this studly, hirsute male's proposal.

Considering all the contributors to intimacy in a relationship, most if not all can be attributed to naturally occurring female traits. In their 2015 report "The State of the American Manager," Gallup showed that people working for female managers are more engaged than those working for male managers. Note that workplace engagement has sucked for decades, so while it's not where we want it (for SO MANY reasons), there's something about female leaders that's worth looking into.

Let's start with **warmth** as a contributor to trust. According to Amy Cuddy et. al. in "Connect, Then Lead" (*Harvard Business Review*, July-August 2013),

> **WARMTH MIGHT BE DIFFICULT TO DESCRIBE IN WORDS, BUT CHANCES ARE YOU KNOW IT WHEN YOU FEEL IT.**

"warmth is the conduit of influence." In other words, if others trust your intentions, they will deeply consider your ideas and guidance. Cuddy recognizes the value of competence and strength, two factors that contribute to trust, but asserts that starting with warmth is paramount to greater success in a relationship. "Prioritizing warmth helps you connect immediately with those around you, demonstrating that you hear them, understand them, and can be trusted by them."

Warmth might be difficult to describe in words, but chances are you know it when you feel it. When someone is warm, you might feel affection, respect, tolerance, friendship, excitement, or love. You have an emotional connection that transcends the confidence you might feel in them due to their overall credibility or reliability. It's the feeling they are both trustworthy and they, in turn, will trust you. People who inspire these feelings are often simply described as warm!

When it comes to leaders, it's important to know that the opposite of warmth isn't the capability, accountability, confidence, intelligence, creativity, and other attributes they bring to their role. Those qualities all coexist and contribute to the trust we develop in our leaders.

However, there is an order in which leaders should manifest their gifts (the numerator on the Trust Model). Characteristics that are markers of credibility and reliability can define the strength and power a leader shows up with. Being strong and powerful can certainly be useful but, when used in lieu of warmth, will likely elicit fear responses in the community. And once fear shows up, the limbic system takes over and people are either figuratively or literally running away. It's our conditioning, and many of us succumb to this subconscious response.

START WITH WARMTH BEFORE DISPLAYING YOUR GIFTS OF CREDIBILITY AND RELIABILITY.

Instead, to be recognized as warm and therefore emotionally connectable, START with warmth before displaying your gifts of credibility and reliability.

Intimacy isn't only about warmth. Another factor is **empathy**, the ability to understand the world through other people's eyes, minds, and hearts. To manage with empathy, leaders need to acquire gobs of self-awareness, whereby they know how their actions make others feel. Empathy is the ability to put yourself in another's shoes, not just think you know how they feel, but actually feel it. Granted, going through the day ALWAYS feeling how others feel would be emotionally exhausting, and leaders have their own feelings, let alone those pesky strategies, visions, and general operations to attend to. However, employing empathy at select times is going to produce better leadership behavior that doesn't promote a culture of fear.

You might be thinking that fear isn't such a bad thing. Motivating through fear can be effective, especially if a leader is the type who doesn't mind winning at the expense of someone else losing. Niccolò Machiavelli, diplomat, politician, historian, philosopher, humanist, writer, playwright, and poet (man, Wikipedia sure is thorough) of the Renaissance period, describes the unscrupulous behavior of leaders—political rulers specifically—who don't hesitate to behave immorally. Acting dishonestly, killing innocents, and generally being ruthless are methods that Machiavelli suggests help tyrants maintain their control. It doesn't take a huge intellectual leap to see where Machiavellian leadership is employed in modern times, and maybe now you're understanding how leading through fear might negatively impact people's trust in leaders.

However, fear is a powerful motivator and can be used to catalyze behavior. For instance, if your company has determined that it's on the brink of bankruptcy, reconfiguring the budget, spending habits, and sales methodologies—like NOW—might save the company and its employees from economic doom. Granted, the fear might inspire some long days and nights, but this is occasionally the urgency that communities must deploy for survival. While fear is quite inspiring, too much is exhausting and morale sapping, and strong leaders choose carefully when to pull it out of the arsenal. If long-term sustainability and the well-being of a community are the goals, fear must be a highly selective tactic as it's a major contributor to the destruction of trust. Fear can occasionally work, but it REALLY sucks for a lot of people.

FEAR REALLY SUCKS FOR A LOT OF PEOPLE.

Back to the building of intimacy—another major contributor is **compassion**. People who are truly compassionate carry their care for others on their sleeves, and the surrounding community knows that their well-being is paramount. Compassion is having a soft spot for others, just caring for the sake of caring, not because of personal gain. Granted, there is a case to be made for a wonderful ROI from living compassionately, but it is best coming from the leader's DNA and not contrived. In fact, all traits described here must be authentic to be functional. Pretending might help for the short term, and there is a case for "faking it 'til you make it," but it's best to get to authenticity as quickly as possible.

Vulnerability is a profound contributor to intimacy. In simplest terms it can be described as being transparent about your mistakes. It can be incredibly

THE FINE ART OF SNUBBING
or how to make people feel like crap

1. Not looking up from your computer when you have a visitor at your desk

2. Telling someone they're not worth their salary

3. Publicly shaming

4. Answering the phone while meeting with someone, or during sex

5. Assigning blame to an individual for organizational or systemic problems

6. Reminding someone that they can be replaced

7. Punishing someone through the assignment of menial tasks

8. Interrupting a conversation, like what you have to say is way better

9. Falling asleep in a presentation, or during sex

10. Avoiding eye contact when passing in the hallway

11. Telling someone that it's too bad the shirt they're wearing didn't come in their size (not in a funny way)

12. Leaving just one member of the team off the party invitation

13. Replacing a stakeholder with someone only on the basis of age, beauty, or body composition

14. Calling someone the wrong name, especially during sex

15. Not communicating with job candidates who didn't get the job

endearing to others, showing your human side and sending a covert yet strong message that it's okay to make mistakes. This, I submit, is a building block of organizational innovation, where the community feels empowered to try new things and make the occasional error. As a business leader, I would occasionally walk around the office and volunteer how I just fucked something up. While I'm trying to mitigate the use of vulgarity in this really important book (aside from, of course, the title), it just so happens that I would say, "You can't believe how I just fucked something up!" So it's a first-person quote, and thus appropriately cited.

It's one thing to demonstrate vulnerability, owning up to your mistakes, and it's entirely another to encourage others to admit their failings. A famous guy in the world of emotional intelligence (whose name is being protected for obvious reasons—I don't need him getting on my case) once wrote about another guy famous for his own understanding and promotion of leadership principles. This other guy strongly emphasized the importance of encouraging his people to take accountability for screwing up. Inspired to get into the fray, I commented about how powerful it might have been for this guy to publicly admit to his own mistakes, modeling the actual behavior he wanted out of his team. This inspired the famous EQ guy to respond to me that his featured guest was transparent about his own mistakes, but didn't mention it in this particular blog post. Oh well. So much for my brush with fame.

YOU CAN'T BELIEVE HOW I JUST FUCKED SOMETHING UP!

While there are other contributors to building intimacy, I will finish with **humility**, after which you'll probably get my drift. Humility is simply knowing that you don't have all the answers and, regardless of your title within the community, behaving as if the playing field is level. If leaders at the top of the organizational hierarchy are truly humble, they might be a bit embarrassed by their lofty titles. In fact, I'm not a big fan of titles, having relabeled my own as The Cheese, Provocateur, Irritant, and Gangster of Love over the years. Certainly, this was all in good fun, but it was also a constant reminder to myself to stay humble and not forget the good luck that enabled me to attain some leadership responsibility throughout my career.

Collectively, these traits that contribute to the establishment of intimacy have been deemed "soft skills" in the past. Going back to my discussion with the group of female leaders, these traits are typically associated with women, who are stereotypically warmer and more nurturing. I submit that these skills are not exclusive to gender, and we can probably ascribe them to people we've known of all genders. (See how enlightened I am? Two genders don't cover the gamut of our sexual identification.) The difference between those who reveal these qualities and those who don't isn't gender, it's courage. In executive forums I've moderated, I asked participants about the fears they may have had about leading with these skills. Here is a list of some of their responses:

"I won't be taken seriously."

"My people will take advantage of me."

"People won't think I'm taking my job seriously."

"I will come across as weak."

"My people won't feel accountable for their own work."

"I will lose people's respect."

When I asked whether these leaders had empirical validation for their fears, I didn't get ANY affirmative responses. As it turned out, "soft skills" were deemed signs of weakness based simply on a belief system and not actual evidence.

It's quite possible that so-called soft skills, when employed without developing, honing, and increasing reliability and credibility, could be perceived as weakness. However, we don't have enough evidence to determine this because the balance in our communities vastly selects for competency. Leaders can show up and spend 100% of their time focusing on intimacy and the balance would still heavily favor competency, because it's so ingrained in the conventional "wisdom" (read dysfunctional paradigm) of the criteria by which leaders are selected.

GIVEN THE STRENGTH OF CONVENTIONAL THINKING AROUND THE EMPLOYMENT OF POWER SKILLS, IT WILL TAKE HEAPING GOBS OF COURAGE TO DEVELOP AND USE THEM.

Knowing how these "soft skills" can build the trust we want within the highest functioning communities, I submit that we should call them "power skills." When employed along with other trust builders, with just the right amount of confidence (more on that later), power skills coexist quite well with credibility and reliability, and create a well-rounded leader who can drive collaboration, innovation, performance, results, well-being, strategy, vision, and all other things that bolster communities, all while holding people accountable for their roles—we can even fire them, if necessary.

Given the strength of conventional thinking around the employment of power skills, it will take heaping gobs of courage to develop and use them. In fact, there are some communities where these skills will be deemed weak, and if you're believing that our communities are in need of help—which most are—then leading where dysfunctional paradigms are stuck may not be a good fit for you. If you want to make a real difference, take two shots of courage, build your intimacy muscles, and find a receptive community to flex them!

While the utilization of comfort foods or mild intoxicants may have helped open your imagination to the possibilities of intimacy, the next chapter on self-interest might be best experienced after dropping acid.

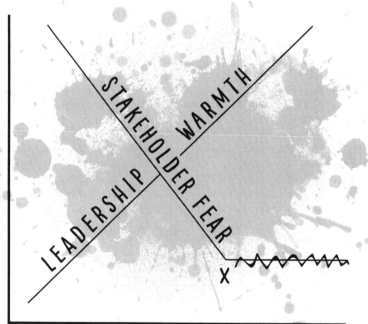

Relationship Between Warmth and Fear

X: Inflection point, because all good graphs have them.

〰〰〰〰 : Can't eliminate fear entirely, because we're so good at feeling it.

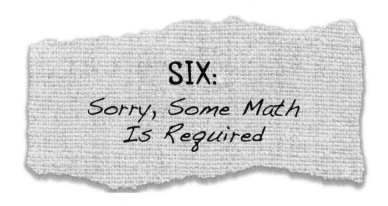

SIX:
Sorry, Some Math Is Required

By now you might be thinking to yourself, "Hey, I have this trust thing down. I can be an effective leader!" Let's revisit our handy Trust Model:

$$T\,(TRUST) = \frac{C\,(CREDIBILITY) + R\,(RELIABILITY) + I\,(INTIMACY)}{S\,(SELF\text{-}INTEREST\ OR\ ORIENTATION)}$$

You have great CREDIBILITY shown by phenomenal credentials decorating your walls, such as your master's diploma in something impressive from an expensive school, framed behind fade-resistant glass, and a certificate in something that lets you decorate your business card with most of the letters of the alphabet. Your credibility doesn't stop there, as you've had news stories written about your great success, and you speak with great confidence, very few "ums" and statements ending without the rising tones usually reserved for questions. Call it executive presence, you put on a pretty good show!

You know how RELIABLE you are, as you don't remember the time you dropped the ball because you simply forgot, and underlings never gave you the feedback that they weren't able to count on you for jack. But you do pretty much answer your requests for lunch, return a lot of your emails, and are rarely more than 30 minutes late for meetings.

And you've got the INTIMACY thing locked down since you've actually read Daniel Goleman's *Emotional Intelligence: Why It Can Matter More Than IQ* and can regurgitate a great definition of EQ. Oh yeah, and you once expressed a real honest feeling while in therapy.

But seriously, maybe you really have mastered the elements found on the numerator of the Trust Model. You have real skills and knowledge. People can count on you to get things done. And you have a wonderfully warm side, are occasionally empathic, and sincerely care about others. So congrats, you have effectively built up the top of the equation.

But don't get too comfortable, buckeroo. Because there's that pesky S in the denominator, and if my math skills are still reasonably intact (I did take 5 quarters of calculus in college and don't remember a single thing), the larger the denominator, the smaller the result—that is, trust.

S IS FOR SELF-INTEREST

From the day I stole Green et. al.'s Trust Model to exploit for my own uses, I've been equating self-interest with ego. Now that I own a copy of *The Trusted Advisor*, I can tell you I'm simpatico with the authors. They also equate self-interest with selfishness, and other descriptors including self-centeredness, self-absorption, conceit, greed, and crossing into the realm of the pathological, narcissism.

Here's the problem with an overly inflated ego: it simply negates all the great stuff found in the numerator of the equation. Trust simply goes poof—and with it, quality relationships. In a conversation with Charlie Green, I posited that everything on the top of the Trust Model doesn't really matter, that it's almost all about the S, and he said he might agree. Of course, it's entirely possible that he had something better to do and just wanted to get me off the phone.

Now ego isn't necessarily a bad thing. We all have one and if it's healthy, it shows up as confidence, conviction, authenticity, and perhaps the impetus to take reasonable risks and make good decisions. It's when confidence spills into the arena of arrogance that things get hairy. Overconfidence, big-headedness, egoism—when expressed with

BIG EGOS MESS THINGS UP.

utter disregard for other people in the room—often earns you a label—you got it, a DICK! And when your interests leave no room for others since you believe you reside squarely at the epicenter of everyone's universe and their existence is designed solely to make your life better, then you might earn the granddaddy of monikers—a FUCKING DICK.

> *A quick reminder regarding political correctness: One might argue that this label is gender specific to males, but I assert that the term is blind to anatomical landmarks, and as such can apply to anyone regardless of gender identification or choice of restrooms.*

Unless you've led an unusually lucky life, chances are awfully good that you've been moved to classify someone as the big FD. If so, hopefully you've resisted the temptation to call them this to their face, though admittedly it can be tempting. The problem is, if you think you might regret it later, it's best to retain your dignity and not lose it at the expense of the lowly dick. While you imagine the scenarios in your past (or present) where a dick has reared their ugly head, here are a few examples from my own life, some of which inspired me to do something about it (like dedicating an entire business around the value of checking one's ego at the door).

PULLING RANK

I was leading a team in the field, conducting marketing, sales, education, and technical support, when a friend on the inside told a story about the company's top executive's autocratic style. He was new with the company, hired from the outside and in the role for about six months, when this incident occurred. The marketing team and this executive were discussing strategy on product development and an issue arose where there was a matter of disagreement. The entire marketing team, representing over 50 years of collective experience, was aligned on the issue and the only dissenter was the top exec. Each member of the marketing team passionately tried to explain why their strategy was the most viable. To resolve the issue, the top executive said, "Okay, everybody take out your business card and tell me what title you have with this company." So much for building respect!

YOUR VOTE DOESN'T MATTER

So I'm sitting in a meeting with the CEO, CFO, Director of Sales, Director of Manufacturing, and Director of Engineering. There's an implant product development initiative the company had been working on for years and we're talking about its future viability. The CFO asserts that the company has no money in the bank to underwrite future R & D, and there's

Don't Be A Fucking Dick Checklist

Stuff I didn't do today:

- ✔ Yell
- ✔ Forget my co-worker's name
- ✔ Took credit for someone else's work
- ✔ Judged someone on the basis of their weight, gender, skin color, age
- ✔ Not listen
- ✔ Point to my credentials as justification to act unilaterally
- ✔ Not pay everyone a living wage
- ✔ Be so serious about everything
- ✔ Take the best parking spot in the employee lot
- ✔ Read email during a meeting
- ✔ Think I was right about everything
- ✔ Forget to use soap in the shower
- ✔ Forget to shower

no pipeline of investment capital on the radar. The Director of Engineering says there isn't a good redesign worthy of consideration, and the current iteration represents undue safety risks to patients. The sales director has been clamoring for additional resources to support the sales effort of products on the shelf, and says if we're investing in something, it should be to assure the success of the current product line. And the manufacturing director expresses frustration that he doesn't have enough resources to purchase raw materials to support the sale of current product. And I sum the whole thing up by re-iterating that to move forward with the R & D project would place too great a risk on the company, and we should either abandon the project or table it for an extended time.

What immediately ensued was the CEO berating the CFO for the company not having enough cash in the bank; in fact, we all must be under the mistaken impression that he was running a democracy. Despite the consensus of opinion held by the company's most senior leaders, he declared that the project was not only to be continued, but accelerated. The critical thinkers in the room were nothing short of incredulous, but not surprised as this style of decision-making had many, many precedents. I retreat to my office and the CEO immediately follows, shuts my door, and with a smug smile asks, "So, how do you think that went?" All I said was it was interesting. It took me many days, if not a couple weeks, to wash that incident off me and I know my coworkers felt the same.

NEITHER DOES YOUR TIME

This anecdote comes from a trusted source in a company that had a president with a flaming ego. He was a raging autocrat and the organization did daily dances around him, trying to keep his temper and questionable decision-making in check. Apparently, he liked to start each week by meeting with his senior leaders, establishing a plan for the week to come. Not a bad idea, actually, to set the tone for the week. But he lost points on execution.

The meeting was called for 8:00 sharp and included about eight people, not including the president, around a conference table. The problem was, the president didn't hold himself accountable to the time and he'd typically arrive late, sometimes up to an hour. It might be reasonable to assume, if it appeared the president was late, people could leave the conference room to start their work and reconvene upon the president's arrival. As logical as this might seem, it was the president's expectation—in fact demand—that nobody was to leave that conference room until he had arrived, so that the meeting could commence the instant he walked in the door. He insisted that people sit there staring at each other, waiting for his highness to conduct the meeting then summarily dismiss them to their waiting tasks. Apparently, and not surprisingly, everybody hated the guy.

STRESS IS DEVELOPMENTAL

I was meeting with a potential client for my career coaching practice, someone who was currently working but suddenly desperate to get out. It turns out he hated, loathed, despised his boss—a theme consistent with many of my clients and, I guess, a lot of other people.

On paper, this guy had a dream job. He was the head of a business unit within his company, accountable for all functional aspects including product development, marketing, sales, and customer service. He had even conjured up a product innovation himself that turned into millions of dollars of revenue for the company. Back to the boss.

The company's owner had the idea that a culture of employee shame, belittlement, and harsh criticism let to the greatest productivity. After about a year on the job, this potential client mustered the nerve to ask his peers in other business units if this style was long-standing. When he heard that these were basic operating principles within the organization, and that the owner and his devotees believed causing such intense stress was developmental, he started to look for a way out.

This prospective client, for the first time in his life, wasn't sleeping well and had recently been diagnosed with stomach ulcers. So I guess you could say this dick of a boss was correct: treating people like crap is developmental—the development of physical illness and loathing.

If you want to add your own story, feel free to do so, using the following template:

There was this person _____
and I couldn't believe my ears when they
_____! Yeah, it was
all about them and they didn't give a crap
about _____. I was so pissed
I wanted to _____.
Nobody trusted this person and had
other choice names for them such as
_____, _____, and
_____. Anybody who had the
opportunity to leave, left. If I ever find
myself working for a _____ like
this again, I might just run off to a deserted island and live off coconuts and insects.

So, how important is this issue, relative to so many others? Organizations have been striving for DECADES to improve culture and stakeholder (including employee) engagement. Statistically, the needle hasn't moved in a very positive direction and, in some instances, has regressed into deeper disengagement, where employees not only aren't passionate, loyal, or decent stewards of the enterprise, but have at least one foot out the door. Turnover is rampant, which is a direct reflection on poor engagement.

An inspiration came to me when reading *The Art of Possibility* by Rosamund and Ben Zander. In the book they describe an organization that has adopted Rule Number Six, which is to not take yourself so seriously. By adhering to this rule, people would lighten up, creating space for fun and humor, allowing them to relax enough so their best talents could manifest. While reading this, it dawned on me that this principle of lightening up is, at best, loosely encouraged in organizations. However, I believe that not only is it vital, it might be the ONLY thing that needs to happen throughout an organization to enable it and its people to thrive. This newfound clarity became the inspiration behind my creating the Institute to Stop Taking Yourself So Seriously! Imagine, an entire enterprise dedicated

> ORGANIZATIONS HAVE BEEN STRIVING FOR DECADES TO IMPROVE CULTURE AND STAKEHOLDER (INCLUDING EMPLOYEE) ENGAGEMENT. STATISTICALLY, THE NEEDLE HASN'T MOVED IN A VERY POSITIVE DIRECTION.

to spreading the message that big egos mess things up, fun and joy are important, and outstanding relationships are vital to supporting the health and well-being of communities. Let's

LET'S ACCEPT THAT YOU MIGHT BE A DICK AND FIGURE OUT A WAY TO BE SOMETHING A BIT MORE TOLERABLE.

start bringing the word "love" into the vernacular of our communities, including business, where it's rarely heard.

Now, one might be asking, why are dicks dicks? To me, any analysis into the causality of dickness is merely an academic exercise, best left to the psychologists and neuroscientists out there. To me, it's not a matter of why. If a person is a dick, yet they want to have and promote good relationships, the onus of excising this sinister characteristic resides squarely on them. The pathway to better communities led by solid leaders is a matter of how. Let's accept that you might be a dick and figure out a way to be something a bit more tolerable.

If you're not convinced that you have the capacity to scare the bajeebers out of someone, venture very delicately into the next chapter. You'll see how easy it is to succumb to an inflated sense of yourself. And if it makes you feel any better, I'll admit that I've been guilty as charged!

SEVEN:
Who's the Fairest?

Maybe you've reached this intentionally irritating chapter thinking to yourself that you have the chops to be an amazing leader. You have heaps of experience, expertise, and cool-sounding titles you've accumulated over the years. You hold yourself accountable and have demonstrated a great capacity for responsiveness and being right at least some of the time. And you've even taken an emotional intelligence assessment that provides empirical evidence that you're not a total moron. Even though all that is great, and you know trust can vaporize in an instant when self-interest is high, you still don't see yourself ever being cannibalized by the part of your brain that sees you as a big motherfucking deal.

> OCCASIONALLY LOSING CONSCIOUS CONTROL OF OUR EGOS IS JUST AN EVERYDAY PART OF THE HUMAN CONDITION.

Well, it might be time to get a better mirror. After we've achieved some success, especially after years of trying, it's commonplace to put ourselves on a pedestal. It takes work to keep our feet firmly grounded, work that I'll discuss later, but no matter how good we are at tempering our enthusiasm for ourselves, occasionally losing conscious control of our egos is just an everyday part of the human condition.

Placing ourselves above others isn't the only way of manifesting egos that compromise trust and relationships. In fact, it's possible that the truly humble reader, someone who isn't outwardly egotistical and self-centered, can nonetheless show up as a bit of an ass. Here are some signs that you might be taking yourself too seriously, starting with the

TERRIBLY UNFUNNY TRIO (TUT) OF DISORDERS:

IT'S HARD TO LAUGH AT YOURSELF.

Whether you need to think you're infallible or you need others to think you're perfect, you simply can't come to grips with the fact that you're often just as ridiculous as the rest of us. You make dumb mistakes, you step in gum, your body makes ungodly (and funny!) noises, and you've had a joke fall flat. Surely that couldn't be you with an enormous hunk of spinach in your teeth, yielding a smile like Captain Hook? No! You can't see any of this as funny because you are incapable of seeing yourself as anything less than hot stuff.

BEING ABLE TO LAUGH AT YOURSELF IS VERY HUMANIZING.

But just like admitting you're wrong, being able to laugh at yourself—out loud and in public—is very humanizing and endearing to those around you. It says, "Hey, I'm one of you! And would you mind lending me a piece of dental floss?" If you've done something silly in public and you don't laugh at yourself, others will naturally feel that your ego might be too tender to be as human as the rest of the people in the room. If you're expecting others to pretend that the comedy didn't happen, that's just magical thinking and authenticity has exited the room. It did happen, it was funny, so get over yourself and let the laughter rip.

YOU CAN'T BE THE BUTT OF A JOKE.

Hand in glove with the inability to laugh at yourself is the refusal to be the butt of a joke. Other people can't laugh at you! Maybe you can laugh at yourself, but if anyone joins in, they've breached an egotistical bulwark. "Hey, I know I can be an occasional doofus, but you are not allowed to either recognize or acknowledge it!"

Often, people who can't take it have the least problem dishing it out. Sure this might reveal nothing more than raging insecurity, nevertheless it appears as jerkiness to others. Sometimes it's not about reality but perception, and as we all know, perception trumps truth. Remember, the world isn't entirely functional; we are, after all, letting our limbic systems run the show.

Letting others playfully tease you is a great equalizer that says we're all in this together: I'm on the team and, in the most important ways, we're equals. It's a display of confidence in yourself when you're willing to engage as the imperfect, quirky person you are. And we all can have some fun with it.

> **YOU NEED TO BE THE FUNNIEST PERSON IN THE ROOM.**

Completing the TUT, this condition doesn't necessarily require an actual sense of humor. Rather, you simply believe you possess one and think it's the dang best, maybe on the planet. Never mind that your family and social circles think you're flat as an amoeba under a microscope, somehow you believe that the people in your leadership sphere find you breathtakingly hilarious. And if they don't laugh at your lame attempts at humor, you take offense and blame them for not getting your clever quips.

There are a couple signs that you may possess this affliction:

1. people laugh when you didn't intend to be funny,

2. people tell you *"you're so funny."*

Note that the latter are either big-time suck ups and ladder climbers or they're simply afraid to incur your ire. (As a cautionary side note, the ladder climbers are often self-serving, and NOT the type of leaders who will be the most effective within your community.)

OTHER SIGNS:

YOU'RE AFRAID TO LOOK STUPID IN FRONT OF A GROUP OF PEOPLE.

I do a fair amount of public speaking and, for some unexplained reason, I occasionally articulate an "r" as a "w." I have no idea what neurological shenanigans are happening, but right before the crowd's eyes, I morph into Elmer Fudd. Luckily, I've gotten over the need to be Mr. Perfect or I'd never be able step to the front of a room. I don't rehearse my talks with the intention of being or appearing super slick. Rather,

THE FEAR OF LOOKING STUPID IS ONE MANIFESTATION OF THE DEEP NEED TO BE RIGHT.

I'm comfortable speaking in a more conversational tone, replete with imperfection and the occasional widiculousness.

On the other hand, some people are deathly afraid of being wrong, flawed, or rough in front of groups. In other words, they are afraid of appearing human. Rather than being accessible, relatable, and like anybody sitting in the economy seats, they must be the absolute authority in the room who will have a definitive answer for each and every question that might come forth. Last I looked, nobody knows everything and the phrase "I don't know" is highly illustrative of courage and humility—two qualities that build trust.

The fear of looking stupid is one manifestation of the deep need to be right. When promoted to a leadership role, this might be the first anxiety-provoking awareness leaders have. The belief that people will start looking to the leader for the truth is probably valid on some levels, as people want guidance that is rooted in sound data and judgment. A delicate balancing act must ensue, whereby humility is infused with confidence and courage, while the leader is seen as occasionally fallible and willing to admit it. NOBODY expects anybody to be perfect, so it's not helpful to expect ourselves to be, or appear, flawless.

YOU NEED TO HAVE THE LAST WORD IN AN ARGUMENT.

This is another behavioral expression of the need to be right. I learned about this as a kid who often argued with my mother, who would typically end the dispute by saying, "Oh sure, you have to have the last word!"—which was a bit ironic, because

> **THE HUMILITY REQUIRED TO UNDERSTAND THAT THERE IS SO MUCH MORE TO TRUTH THAN WHAT RESIDES IN YOUR HEAD REQUIRES INCREDIBLE BRAVERY.**

those were usually the last words uttered in our spirited arguments.

Needing to be right probably comes to us naturally, honestly, and easily. As a society that places great credence in the value of being smart, noted by our willingness (at least in the United States) to throw over 100 thousand dollars into undergraduate degrees, we think it's important to know stuff. To not know stuff is a challenge in life, as it's very comforting to settle on any truth, even a made-up one, to help make sense of the world around us. Of course, this might have very little to do with facts, as evidenced by the last political discussion you had with someone of differing beliefs.

The humility required to understand that there is so much more to truth than what resides in your head requires incredible bravery. While we often get better at this with age (thank goodness my kids are now past their teens), it's never too soon to contemplate your factual deficiencies in service of your relationships.

Ironically, needing to get the last word in an argument might indicate your doubts in the merits of your case. The last word is akin to kicking the game-winning field goal with one second on the game clock, leaving the opposing team no chance to come back. The only difference is that, in real life, the game is not necessarily over, and you're just left pretending that you won the argument. Any deficiencies behind the logic in your case endure, as does your appearance as an overbearing blowhard.

YOU'RE INCREDIBLY IMAGE CONSCIOUS.

We all have an image of ourselves. It shows up in the way we dress, the language we use, the hairstyles we wear, and the cars we drive. Advertising executives know this all too well, appealing to our self-images by positioning largely generic products—think vodka, shoes, cell phones, and boxer briefs—to align with our ideas of ourselves. Are you a worldly soul, gym rat, or tech trendsetter? Then, have we got something for you! The Peanuts cartoon character Snoopy had an alter ego known as Joe Cool, portrayed as a dude leaning back, arms folded, sporting dark sunglasses. Yes, even a beagle can think of himself as a cool cat, when he's really still a dog.

DEALING WITH A BIT OF AN IDENTITY CRISIS IS HEALTHY

Despite being woefully similar in such fundamental ways, humans also like to "run their number." But if we push it too much, everyone knows we're just trying too hard. This puts up a wall between people, denying enough closeness to talk, listen, care, and collaborate. The space for trust is diminished as running your number too loudly shows a big capacity for inauthenticity. After all, underneath all the tattoos, designer clothes, monstrous deltoid muscles, French berets, crazy expensive tennis shoes, "I'm With Stupid" tee shirts, hundred-dollar blow dries, and "I Voted" buttons lie people who have ludicrous bed head, breath to stun dogs, pieces of food clinging to their lips, and farts producing any of a number of untoward consequences.

I wonder if always dealing with a bit of an identity crisis is healthy, grounding us in the flawed humanity that is a common denominator of every connected, functional community.

YOU OFFEND VERY EASILY.

If you're still reading this, clearly you've gotten past the title of the book, a good sign that you have the patience, tolerance, and acceptance to give people the room to express themselves, maybe in ways that you wouldn't necessarily choose for yourself. Nevertheless, there are people who take offense at the use of profanity, and they wouldn't take a whack at this book and enjoy the magical ideas contained herein.

Taking offense can be a way that people inspire change in others' behavior. When a politician says or tweets something offensive to many, an uprising of indignation can bring politicians back in alignment with the mainstream. Movements have begun as a result of the reaction from public comments, which can stimulate an advancement in human evolution.

However, it's one thing to be personally hurt by a verbal or written attack, in which case providing a defense is often a reasonable reaction. It's another to claim offense without personal hurt, setting the stage to argue merely for argument's sake, which is an exercise in futility. It's all about authenticity, one of the bases of trust-building where emotional intelligence rules the day.

IF YOU DON'T WANT TO BE A DICK, IT'S HELPFUL TO KNOW WHEN YOU'RE LOOKING LIKE ONE.

People grow up with all sorts of rules, rules conveyed by authority figures that we never thought could be challenged. However, rules change or were crummy from the get-go, and they're worthy of scrutiny. So using the word "fuck" in a safe, non-accusatory way isn't meant to cause a hurt feeling. Calling somebody a fucking idiot, with the intent to cause hurt, is another story. In the case of this book, insinuating that someone can be perceived as a fucking dick is not meant to cause hurt, but to provide the insight that other people might see you that way. If you don't want to be a dick, it's helpful to know when you're looking like one.

The phrase "like water off a duck's back" has seemingly been lost in this era of taking things so seriously. I propose that we bring it back into our daily vernacular, letting things roll off when they aren't intended to be hurtful.

YOU SNUB PEOPLE FOR THE MOST FAMOUS PERSON IN THE ROOM.

We humans want to be important and may judge ourselves by the company we keep. At social or work gatherings, we may be engaged in conversation with peers when into our midst walks the boss or other celebrity. Some may disrupt their conversation in order to engage with the more famous person, leaving peers feeling disregarded and hurt. Or when the celebrity is engaged in conversation, some might not hesitate to interrupt, usurping the conversation. Obviously, this social faux pas, the need to associate with important people at the cost of treating others with disrespect, does not play well.

Here's what a snubee might be feeling when a snubber abandons them for someone more popular:

I'm clearly not that important to you.

Maybe I'm not that interesting to you.

My feelings are less important than your need to feel important.

I was just going to ask to marry you, but I guess that can wait for another time—and another person.

On the other hand, maintaining focus on your discourse with a peer, friend, or coworker and choosing that focus over the opportunity to brush with a famous person, is highly enchanting and conjures trust, loyalty, and collegiality. Choosing to build trust over your need for self-importance is great for you and for the community. By the way, there doesn't need to be a third person involved to snub someone. A cell phone or computer could usurp your attention from another person. This dynamic occurs all the time in coffee shops where two people invite the rest of their world to the meeting by keeping an eye out for—and often responding to—texts, emails, and calls. Simply not being present in the moment is a way of telling someone they're not important or interesting enough to capture your undivided attention—a social hurt that is felt in the brain as profoundly as a punch in the nose.

If you want to be a better snubber, please refer to the chart on page 50. My cheap ploy to keep you rummaging through this book.

YOU USUALLY SUCCUMB TO AN IRRESISTIBLE URGE TO GIVE UNSOLICITED ADVICE.

One weakness of the human condition is that because we love our own ideas so much, we believe other people must love them too. The best ideas are our own; any whisper of disagreement can incite what looks like oppositional behavior. If you've ever raised a kid, or been one yourself, you know how this works. Just tell a kid to do something and they'll resist, regardless of how good the idea might be, only because they've been told to do it.

MOST OFTEN, WE NEED OUR BEST IDEAS TO ORIGINATE INTRINSICALLY, DERIVED FROM OUR VALUES AND DESIRES.

The older person's (not to be confused with adult's) subconscious reaction is often triggered by the reception of unsolicited advice. There are theories about why people give unasked for, and often unwanted, advice such as a need for power and control, or to alleviate chronic psychological distress (how great is Google?!). But those theories are beside the point—nobody likes to be told what to do, yet some people are masters at shouting out their wisdom upon largely deaf ears.

Most often, we need our best ideas to originate intrinsically, derived from our values and desires. Making choices based on our own thoughts and experiences provides necessary personal ownership, consistent with our basic need for autonomy. Certainly, there are times when a bit of unsolicited advice can come in handy, like "Hey, that hamburger is contaminated with E. coli," or "Stopping on those railroad tracks might be bad for your and your car's health."

EXHAUSTIVE LIST OF PEOPLE,
SINCE THE INCEPTION OF
RECORDED TIME, WHO HAVE SAID
"Thanks for the unsolicited advice."

> **YOU CHOOSE THE COLORFUL SPRINKLED DONUT OVER THE LESS JUVENILE OPTION, ONLY WHEN NOBODY ELSE IS LOOKING.**

Admittedly, this one might be a bit esoteric and is simply a theory I've been working on for a few decades. In my years in the surgical device industry, it was customary to bring baked goods to the operating room staff and surgeons, helping to keep their blood sugar elevated enough to dissuade them from yelling at you. As an operating room leader, it's sometimes hard to let your adult façade down, especially if you're taking yourself especially seriously in this occasionally stressful environment—which is in some ways a good thing, but it can go too far. Egos, to say the least, were often front and center.

Being of a rather childlike mindset myself (as if you're surprised), I made certain that a good percentage of the sweets were topped with multicolored sprinkles because I just think they're more fun. My local bakery came to understand that when I placed an order for dozens of donuts, they were to create the "juvenile assortment"—lots of color and, in my view, entertainment. Of course, there were also smatterings of maple, peanut, chocolate-iced, and plain pastries, just so people had choice.

I made it my own experiment to note people's selections, and I got the sense that the people more in touch with their youthful selves took the colored sprinkles, while the more serious took the more adult-looking delicacies. My own non-scientific analysis also concluded that some people took the technicolor items only when other people weren't looking. Even though you won't find this particular study in any peer-review journal, and it certainly lacks credibility, it nevertheless could be true.

The point of these signs is that all of us can easily enter the territory of taking ourselves too seriously. If you don't recognize that you are, at least occasionally, guilty of some of these signs, a few exercises in self-awareness might be in order. I know that I've been an offender and that, when I'm doing a poor job of being who I want to be, I'll blunder into excessive gravity. Because it's so easy to fall victim to our natural inclination to think too highly of ourselves, the next chapter may provide some strategies to catch ourselves before we win the fucking dick trophy.

> ALL OF US CAN EASILY ENTER THE TERRITORY OF TAKING OURSELVES TOO SERIOUSLY.

EIGHT:
The Ol' One-Two

Trying to eliminate unwanted habits, or develop new ones, can make for a very clumsy dance. Volumes have been written about techniques to make and break habits and countless experts have been recruited to help. Consultants, coaches, psychotherapists, hypnotists, physicians, policy-makers, parents, counselors, judges, teachers, motivational speakers, coworkers, siblings, and pharmacists are just some of the people we might recruit to help us make positive, lasting changes. I don't know what percentage of the Gross Domestic

> *CHANGING HABITS, WHILE POTENTIALLY DAUNTING, IS NONETHELESS ENTIRELY ACHIEVABLE. SIMPLIFICATION IS TANTAMOUNT TO SUCCESS.*

Product is dedicated to personal improvement, but it's probably right up there with the ice cream and pizza markets, feeding two habits that ought not to be messed with.

Changing habits, while potentially daunting, is nonetheless entirely achievable. To my way of thinking, the more complicated you make it, the harder it will be and the better it is for all the experts waiting in line to help you make a habit of paying them boatloads of cash. Simplification is tantamount to success, even if you are facing a strong physiological or psychological addiction to substances or behaviors. Yes, there are times when a little outside help is called for, and the professionals needn't worry that this chapter will put them out of work. My little two-step process, though, is definitely a reasonable first-line attempt at becoming the person you want to be:

STEP 1.

Decide that you want to change a habit.

Honestly, this isn't a one-time decision that you'll be making. Rather, it will be a series of minute-by-minute, hour-by-hour, day-by-day, week-by-week, month-by-month, and year-by-year choices. Remember the big part of your brain that operates on autopilot? Well, this bully is constantly competing with your thinking, choosing, intentional brain, often hijacking your plans to do better. The importance of seizing conscious control is no better illustrated than with the dietary choices you want to make in the face of all the alluring fat, sugar, and salt readily at hand. No wonder weight loss books and programs are key elements of personal budgets, because it's so dang hard to stick with a program long enough to make it a life-long practice. (As a trained exercise physiologist, don't get me started on the creation of dietary fads, unsustainable from my point of view yet great for people in the weight loss industry with mortgage payments.)

KEEP MAKING THE SAME DEFINITIVE DECISION.

Sometimes it takes time to get yourself to the point that you've made a definitive decision to change habits, and be ready to act on it. The change process starts with getting enough information to understand options, learning enough to know which is best, and mustering up the courage and energy to take the plunge. A decision made too quickly might not survive the scrutiny of other options that may come your way, enabling you to abandon your best intentions. Take some time, make an informed decision, go for it, and then keep making the same definitive decision!

THE CHANGE PROCESS STARTS WITH GETTING ENOUGH INFORMATION TO UNDERSTAND OPTIONS, LEARNING ENOUGH TO KNOW WHICH IS BEST, AND MUSTERING UP THE COURAGE AND ENERGY TO TAKE THE PLUNGE.

Part of this decision is that it requires 100% commitment from the get-go. You are all in, not 90, 95, or 99 percent on board. You have to agree with yourself that NOTHING is going to derail you because there will be many, many temptations to get you off track.

You get sick, you take vacation, you have a couple drinks, you tell yourself that, just this one time, you're going to stray from your commitment... Nope. Hold steadfast come hell or high water. Of course, you might have a little digression on your way, but with 100% commitment, you'll feel guilty enough hopefully to get yourself back to your goal.

STEP 2.

Remember that you've decided to make a change.

Making a definitive decision is a conscious process, using the intentional thinking part of the brain. If you recall from earlier in this book, the subconscious part of your brain is the autopilot that so easily and quickly usurps control of the conscious part. So ingrained into our normal human condition, it requires a bit of superhuman power to override, but not so much power that it's impossible. It's not.

> *IF YOU CAN JUST REMEMBER THE CHANGES YOU'VE FULLY COMMITTED TO MAKING, YOU ARE WELL ON YOUR WAY TO SUCCESS.*

If you can just remember the changes you've fully committed to making, you are well on your way to success. It is so easy to forget, though, when an intense emotion inspires a dysfunctional reaction. Anger, disappointment, frustration all can overpower conscious intention but the greatest distractor of all is fear. And fear is one of those emotions that humans are woefully inadequate at identifying, as it can manifest in so many ways. Short of therapy to manage fear, there are, nevertheless, effective strategies for remembering.

THE PAUSE

Before, during, or after an exchange, taking a split second to say to yourself something like "I am going to behave in a way that's consistent with my goals" helps move your brain processing from the unconscious to the conscious. My coaching certification employs a technique where the self-talk is "I see this person as fully capable and creative" before every coaching session. It calms down any bias and judgment that may show up in my coaching, and mitigates the urge to provide unsolicited advice. At first, I thought it was a little hokey to do this, but dang it if it doesn't work. Like, every time.

THE ACCOUNTABILITY PARTNER

It's helpful to involve other people in your quest to make a fundamental change. You'll want a real friend, one who'll give you the brutally honest feedback necessary to grow your self-awareness. People who'll tell you stuff to make you feel better aren't going to instigate the necessary discomfort vital to success.

This is where some trained help can come in. Consultants, coaches, therapists, managers, clergy, and maybe an insightful hair stylist can help. Hey, those 45 minutes captive in the salon chair make for some quality time!

THE CONTINUING EDUCATION

A consistent infusion of information will help align your energy around your intended work. There are myriad sources of information; you decide which resonate with your assessment of the truth. Books, journals, magazines, LinkedIn feeds, seminars, YouTube videos, TED Talks—you can't help but stumble upon information that will validate your desired changes, and make you even more popular at social gatherings. There aren't enough hours in a lifetime to absorb the literature around emotional intelligence, so don't drive yourself too crazy trying to find the definitive source or irrefutable data.

THE HIGH-TECH TICKLER

We now have all sorts of battery-powered devices to help us manage our days and annoying social media posts. Technology can play a supporting role in the habit changes you're seeking, but they probably aren't enough to provide all the reminders you'll need to make great new habits stick. The novelty and battery life just don't seem to last for very long.

Think mobile phones and wearable fitness trackers, gizmos you can program with reminders and count your steps toward goal achievement. Sign up for daily motivational messages, create calendar nudges, or set alarms to rouse your conscious brain. Too bad we don't (yet) have implantable devices that sense when we're about to be a dick and proactively jolt us with 200 volts.

TOO BAD WE DON'T (YET) HAVE IMPLANTABLE DEVICES THAT SENSE WHEN WE'RE ABOUT TO BE A DICK AND PROACTIVELY JOLT US WITH 200 VOLTS.

THE LOW-TECH CUE

This is the actual or virtual Post-it Note in your day. Plaster your refrigerator with messages that remind you of your intentions, stick reminders in your car or office, and keep books visible with titles that help inspire your best self. Similar to a fitness tracker, a simple silicon wrist band can be a memory trigger, and may inspire a conversation with a curious questioner compelling you to articulate the goals you're working on. Nothing like going public with all of this! And you can check out the Institute website, www.dontbeafuckingdick.com to buy your very own wristband emblazoned with "DBAFD." Many colors will be available, guaranteed to clash with every day's attire.

One of the best low-tech triggers would be to gift this book to anyone you think could benefit from the message to Not Take Yourself So Seriously! It'll look great on coffee tables and desktops and in boardrooms, the Halls of Congress, and the Oval Office. Maybe buy a few more copies for yourself to strew around the house, as the cover alone keeps this provocative message in the forefront of your consciousness.

THE FISCALLY-PAINFUL EXPERIENCE

We humans are wonderfully complex creatures and one thing that amazes me is the value we place on things that cost us money: The more cost associated with something, the higher the value. We like a return on investments so if we cough up some cash, we might not forget, or altogether abandon, our resolve to change.

One of the best ways to part with some meaningful cash is with other people. This is where the consultants, coaches, and therapists come in. Look, they have bills to pay, and since you're now committed to regarding other people more highly, this is a win-win solution.

THE CONTEMPLATION OF YOUR MORTALITY

Not to be morbid here, but it's always helpful to recall that our days are limited. There's going to be a time when you realize EVERYTHING you thought

IT'S ALWAYS HELPFUL TO RECALL THAT OUR DAYS ARE LIMITED.

was so dang important—including yourself—pales in comparison to simply living a decent, purpose-driven life. Stop and ask yourself, "In 50 years, am I going to care so much about this that I'm willing to trash another person's self-esteem, confidence, or happiness in order to achieve it?" You might find you treat people a bit differently.

THE CONSIDERATION OF YOUR LEGACY

In line with contemplating your mortality is thinking about how you want to be remembered. What life lessons do you want to leave to your survivors, including your family, community, coworkers, students, and constituents? It's helpful to write your obituary, etching in your mind the person you want others to remember.

I conduct a workshop where the final exercise is writing one's own epitaph. In a very short phrase, how would you want future generations to know you, simply by reading your gravestone? I'd want mine to say, "Howie gave a shit."

THE EXTRINSIC REWARD

There's a reason the finest species on the planet, the canine, is typically rewarded with a tasty treat after they've exhibited a desired behavior. As you catch yourself achieving the changes you've set out to make, go ahead and give yourself a tangible reward. As previously mentioned, life is short and it's important to occasionally indulge yourself in the many pleasures at hand.

So simple on paper, so a-bit-more-complicated in real life, the two-step process of habit change will take some energy, but it is a foolproof move toward better leadership. After some time, new ways of being and relating to others will become more natural and automatic. As a note of caution, humans aren't perfect and momentary lapses are to be expected. However, the more people know your positive intention, the more tolerant they'll be for the occasional indiscretion.

> *THE MORE PEOPLE KNOW YOUR POSITIVE INTENTION, THE MORE TOLERANT THEY'LL BE FOR THE OCCASIONAL INDISCRETION.*

If you fear being relegated to a life of eternal dickdom, you can do something about it by just thinking better. Ultimately, this whole personal change thing is an exercise in getting comfortable with discomfort. Operating from the conscious part of your brain can lead to self-criticism, acknowledging your imperfections, and starting to accept the messiness of the human condition. Don't be so hard on yourself, because as I've said before, LIFE IS SHORT! Take a look at some of the ideas in the following chapter to help you lighten up and have more fun, no matter what community you're engaging with. Who knows? You could become very popular!

NINE:
Am I, or Am I Not?

At this time, you might be thinking I've wasted a perfectly good hour of your time. Or if some of the ideas here put you into such a dizzying funk it required professional intervention, then maybe a few weeks went down the drain.

If you believe this book was written for someone else, chances are your own self-awareness is lagging just a bit. The point of Chapter Seven was to show how easy it is to lapse into a zone of too much seriousness. Granted, taking yourself a bit too seriously doesn't necessarily earn you the fucking dick badge, but since it's so easy to have the intentional parts of your thinking hijacked, it's always worth considering.

None of us is perfectly self-aware, and it behooves us to continually seek feedback to see how we're doing. The only exception to this guidance would be if you sincerely think it's good for your community that your ego is manifest in ways that are destructive to relationships. And to you I say, "What a dick!"

If we believe, by now, that healthy communities drive better results, then the overly egotistical leader is likely not getting the results they want. If the FD hasn't considered this notion by now, then either reread this book or check yourself in for electric shock therapy, a lobotomy, or a one-way trip to an uninhabited island.

Perfection isn't the goal. The vast majority of us occasionally lapse into dickness, and if we don't, we might be taking things too cautiously. If we're pushing the envelopes of creativity, productivity, fundamental change, and challenging convention, it's a good bet we get blindsided by goals and the passion that can sometimes interfere with our best intentions. Again, welcome to the human condition!

IT'S VITAL THAT WE EXERCISE COMPASSION AND EMPATHY FOR OURSELVES, DESPITE THE OCCASIONAL TRANSGRESSION FROM OUR BEST INTENTIONS

The good news is, if you work hard on intentionally checking the worst parts of your ego at the door, you will have built up enough social capital that occasional lapses won't harm the community you want to have thrive. My wife recently asked me, "How can someone writing a book on not being a dick sometimes be a dick?" Well, we've been together for over 35 years, we're still married, and my kids pick up my phone calls, so I rest my case.

Life is challenging at almost every step and it's vital that we exercise compassion and empathy for ourselves, despite the occasional transgression from our best intentions. Our time on the planet is about a millisecond compared to the timeline of history, and it's helpful to take as lighthearted approach as possible to life, relaxing, enjoying others, being physically and emotionally comfortable, and simply not taking too much to heart. There's so much out there that we can't change, let alone parts of ourselves that are driven by our deepest, subconscious brains. So, when given the opportunity, LIGHTEN UP!

In an effort to help you gain a healthy perspective, and lighten up whenever possible, I leave you with some of my rules for living a lighthearted, joyous life:

HOWIE'S RULES FOR LIGHTENING UP

1. Remember that life is short and you'll ultimately be dying alone, probably poorly dressed.

2. Don't go into a meeting with a full bladder.

3. When in doubt, or not, have a little something to eat.

4. Unless everyone around you is colorblind, wear a little—or a lot—of vibrant clothing.

5. It's okay, even helpful, to think of funny stuff at funerals.

6. Never be more than 90 seconds away from the nearest piece of dental floss. One exception to this is if you are drawn to corn on the cob, in which case the distance shortens to 60 seconds.

7. Never, ever, ever, ever work for megalomaniacs, psychopaths, or sociopaths, no matter how much money you'd make.

8. Don't tell other people that they're dicks, unless they ask. Rather, sneak a copy of this book onto their desks under the cover of night or anonymously through the mail.

TEN:
Stop Me Before I Write Again

I'm having a hard time finishing this book, because new thoughts continue to find their way into my head. To conclude I'd like to offer a bit more perspective as you might, at this point, be thinking about how you will successfully lead, or whether you're even a leader in the first place.

One thing about advanced emotional intelligence is that it enables you to recognize that you have hurt another person's feelings, and to acknowledge to that person that you've cavalierly mishandled their emotions. Telling someone you're sorry, with contrition and earnestness, goes a long way toward helping the other person start the healing and—hopefully—forgiveness processes.

However, telling someone that you didn't mean to do or say the hurtful thing is not only dismissive of the other person's feelings, it's actually not true. In fact, a part of your brain, whether in your consciousness or buried deeply in some gray matter, directed you to act hurtfully and you must take ownership. "I didn't mean it" doesn't belong in the lexicon of ways we make ourselves feel better for trashing someone else. You did mean it, even though you might regret it. If you immediately regret it before even receiving negative feedback from others, it speaks to the need to pause before acting irrationally, giving yourself a few seconds to think through the possible consequences of your actions. To the question of whether or not you're a leader—leaders don't really need to have titles that traditionally confer leadership: president, manager, executive director, chief snake wrangler. Powerful leadership happens when anyone takes the initiative to influence positive change, new thinking, or constructive disruption. Dismal leadership happens when unhealthy egos rule the day. One of my coaching clients came to me out of utter job dissatisfaction owing to a hyper-negative, controlling, conniving, manipulating, and abusive coworker. He wasn't her boss, but he did have profound influence. When he finally met his vocational demise, within 48 hours my client reported feeling as deeply engaged and enthusiastic with her work as she had ever been. This coworker, while not her boss, lead enormous negativity in my client's workplace.

So as long as you have the time, power, and inclination to impact anyone in any way, you are acting in a leadership capacity. It's your choice whether you want to be a leader who inspires trust.

> *POWERFUL LEADERSHIP HAPPENS WHEN ANYONE TAKES THE INITIATIVE TO INFLUENCE POSITIVE CHANGE, NEW THINKING, OR CONSTRUCTIVE DISRUPTION.*

Finally, a last word on my choice of the word "fuck" in the title of this book. I know it's provocative, and intentionally so. Having heard the phrase enough times in the past, I can't claim to have made it up, but I can claim to have either the courage or stupidity to put it out there, front and center. What I worry about is that the message, in and of itself, is so complete that people might not feel the need to delve into the community health message that is so vital to our individual and communal well-being. So, if you've read this book in its entirety, THANK YOU! And for those of you who are still taking offense, well, fuck you.

ACKNOWLEDGMENTS
It Takes a Village, er, Community!

I am lucky to have countless people in my life who are so willing to help, or at least tolerate, me. This book could not have been written without all the leaders who intentionally or inadvertently allowed me to observe and assess their impacts on communities. Many of these leaders had traditional titles, many had titles that didn't directly signify their place in an organization's hierarchy, and many didn't have a title at all—they simply exerted influence. From companies to nonprofit organizations, and boardrooms to volunteer committees, leaders were everywhere. Some of the most fascinating (to me, at least) of my insights arose in medical clinics, hospitals, and—in particular—hundreds of operating rooms, where the dynamics of surgical teams were profoundly influenced by surgeons. They were authentic, transparent, and sometimes delightfully self-unaware, which enabled my epiphany that emotional intelligence REALLY matters.

Being a dad and husband was also hugely developmental for me. My three beautiful and smart children taught me volumes. Sam, Nate, and Sophie grew up fiercely determined to be true to themselves, and they continue to succeed in this world without selling out. My courageous and inspiring wife, Gail, herself a writer and college professor with a gift for enlightening students on the value of the written word, provides me with the honest, accurate, and sometimes painful feedback that everyone could use in their lives. That is, if they care how they're impacting others around them.

I'm also fortunate to have a large body of research, journals, and books that provided deeper insights into the human condition, many making incredibly compelling cases and written so convincingly that I believed them. A natural skeptic, I didn't have to buy into this stuff, but I did.

Creating the Institute to Stop Taking Yourself So Seriously! and becoming a speaker and author has required an amazing cast of characters. First, my friend Scott "Woody" Woodworth, CEO/Designer at Loudmouth, refused to let the charter of my enterprise go unchallenged. Not only did he help me think better, he and his company continue to let me show up in front of audiences and announce my brand even before I open my mouth. To my many friends, about 30% of whom disliked the title of the book and 70% of whom liked it, thank you for unwittingly participating in my focus groups.

The illustrations in this book are from the amazing mind and hand of my friend from high school days,

Marty Harris. Many people know Marty for his depth and breadth of artistry, but I am particularly indebted for his helping shape my perspective on life. From my most formative years, Marty's insights have been ingrained into my own vernacular, supporting my choice to look at things through funny glasses.

My editor, Gabrielle Dane, provided some spectacular tweaks and taught me more about syntax and punctuation. Charlie Green, who piqued my curiosity with his company's trust model, graciously let me make it my own and a cornerstone of this book. So much more than black ink on white paper, my fabulous book designer (and niece), Shira Atakpu, gave it the look and feel that was so important to the experience I wanted to provide to readers. She is also an accomplished book cover artist, and I think it's most fair to her that you don't judge her covers by the book.

Lastly, and so enormously importantly, I express my eternal gratitude to my friend, confidant, and co-conspirator in challenging conventional thinking, Ronn Lehmann. Ronn, himself an author, suffered through every step of this book's writing, one chapter at a time, making certain that my voice remained apparent and authentic, balancing my desire to entertain readers with the need to get a serious message across. Without his support, encouragement, and provocation, this book's readers would instead probably be catching up on their Calvin and Hobbes anthologies right now.

TO WRITE THE ANNOYING AUTHOR

If, for some reason, you haven't had enough of Howie, you can contact him at Howie@lightenupatwork.com.

Made in the
USA
Lexington, KY